Mark Ibbotson
Bryan Stephens

T0343093

Business
START-UP 2

Workbook

CAMBRIDGE
UNIVERSITY PRESS

CAMBRIDGE
UNIVERSITY PRESS

University Printing House, Cambridge CB2 8BS, United Kingdom

One Liberty Plaza, 20th Floor, New York, NY 10006, USA

477 Williamstown Road, Port Melbourne, VIC 3207, Australia

4843/24, 2nd Floor, Ansari Road, Daryaganj, Delhi – 110002, India

79 Anson Road, #06–04/06, Singapore 079906

Cambridge University Press is part of the University of Cambridge.

It furthers the University's mission by disseminating knowledge in the pursuit of education, learning and research at the highest international levels of excellence.

www.cambridge.org
Information on this title: www.cambridge.org/9780521672085

© Cambridge University Press 2006

First published 2006

Reprinted 2017

Printed in Italy by Rotolito Lombarda S.p.A.

A catalogue record for this publication is available from the British Library

ISBN 978-0-521-67208-5 Workbook with CD-ROM / Audio CD
ISBN 978-0-521-53469-7 Student's Book
ISBN 978-0-521-53470-3 Teacher's Book
ISBN 978-0-521-53471-0 Audio Cassettes (2)
ISBN 978-0-521-53472-7 Audio CDs (2)

Contents

Introduction

Welcome to *Business Start-up* Workbook 2.

There are 12 units in the Workbook to match the 12 units in the Student's Book.

The Workbook is designed for self-study. There is an answer key for the exercises and transcripts of the listening activities at the back of the book.

Reading and writing activities

There is a wide range of activities (puzzles, word searches, anagrams and other exercise types) to give you new and different practice of the grammar and vocabulary in the Student's Book. There's also the chance for you to practise writing emails, memos and other types of business correspondence. You can do the activities in the Workbook after you have finished the corresponding unit in the Student's Book.

Listening activities

There is a CD with listening and speaking exercises for each unit. All these activities are 'hands free'. This means, for example, that you can listen to them in the car, or on a personal CD player, without looking at the Workbook. Most of the speaking activities have an example to listen to first. There are pauses for you to speak, and afterwards you hear a model answer.

The CD-ROM

You can also use the CD on your computer as a CD-ROM. There are extra exercises for every lesson and more chances for you to practise the language that you are learning in class.

1 | Introductions

1 Make sentences.

1 She / responsible / marketing / department.
   She's responsible for the marketing department.

2 He / manage / six / technicians.

   ----

3 They / report / sales / manager.

   ----

4 You / charge / project.

   ----

5 We / deal / financial / problems.

   ----

6 I / look / important / customers.

   ----

2 You are in a meeting in the UK. Introduce yourself and talk about your job and responsibilities (or a job you'd like to do). Make notes to help you remember what to say in English. Write up to 50 words.

   Good morning. My name's ...

   ----

3 Correct the mistakes.

1 Where's the factories?
   Where are the factories?

2 They has offices in London and Rome.

   ----

3 Our factory aren't near Bristol.

   ----

4 Our customers is mainly from Europe.

   ----

5 This year there's 300 companies at the trade show.

   ----

6 We exports our products all over the world.

   ----

7 Does you work in London?

   ----

4 **Complete the puzzle. All the words contain the letter 'D'.**

¹P	R	O	V	I		E	

1 Our engineers ..._provide_.. a good after-sales service.
2 We _____ the equipment in our office in Liverpool.
3 We always meet our customers' _____ .
4 They _____ the parts for free.
5 The company _____ parts for rollercoasters.

5 **Make four sentences. Use phrases from each box.**

Our engineers install	deliver our	provide a	Italy.
We supply spare	the equipment and	to its customers in	24-hour service.
We	exports equipment	our customers all	over the world.
The company	parts to	software products	by air.

1 _Our engineers install the equipment and provide a 24-hour service._
2 _____
3 _____
4 _____

6 **You have a meeting with a company in the UK. Present your company (or a company you know) and its products and services. Make notes to help you do the presentation in English. Write up to 50 words.**

_____
_____
_____
_____
_____

7 **Find food words. Then write them next to the pictures.**

P	A	E	C	O	A	C	C	O	F
S	A	L	A	D	P	A	H	A	O
L	M	E	R	P	P	P	R	I	P	C
A	K	M	R	O	L	R	C	P	N
E	A	N	O	L	E	B	K	L	P
K	(P	O	T	A	T	O)	E	A	O
L	E	A	P	M	N	T	N	K	C
A	A	P	L	B	C	H	I	C	K
B	S	I	W	H	B	F	I	S	H

3 ....

4 ....

5 ....

1 .....*potato*.....

6 ....

2 ....

7 ....

8 ....

8 **Fill in the gaps.**
1 to reserve a table = to ..*book*.. a table
2 the list of food and drink in a restaurant = the ....
3 the biggest dish of the meal = the ....
4 the first dish of a meal = the ....
5 the last dish of a meal = the ....
6 what you pay after a meal = the ....

9 **Match the pairs to make sentences.**

1 Can I have soup   a a reservation.
2 I'd like steak for   b strawberries, please.
3 We have   c bill, please?
4 I don't want   d a starter, just a main course.
5 The same   e for the starter?
6 Could I have the   f like anything else?
7 For dessert, I'd like   g for me, please.
8 Would you   h the main course.

2 | Teamwork

1 **Fill in the gaps in the conversation.**

A How's it going? _Is_ the printer _working_ now? (work)

B Yes.

A Good. So, what _____ you _____ at the moment? (print)

B I _____ a copy of my report. (print)

A OK. Just in time. The man from UPS _____ in reception. (wait)

2 **Make questions for these answers.**

1 _Is the engineer repairing the lift?_

   Yes, the engineer's repairing the lift.

2 _____

   No, the builders aren't working this morning.

3 _____

   I'm planning the budget.

4 _____

   No, the men from the phone company aren't working today.

5 _____

   Yes, the architect's planning the renovation.

6 _____

   No, the builders aren't working to schedule.

7 _____

   Yes, I'm paying a lot for the design changes.

3 **Write a short progress report about a project or job you are working on at the moment. Say how things are going. Write up to 50 words.**

> ▢▢▢
>
> **To:**
> **From:**
> **Subject:** Progress report
>
> _At the moment I'm ..._
> _____
> _____
> _____
> _____
> _____

4 **Complete the sentences. The missing words all contain the letter 'C'.**

1 She speaks very well. She's a good _communicator_ .

2 She has lots of new ideas. She's very ....

3 She's very sure of herself. She's very ....

4 She thinks quickly. She's good at making ....

5 She's 48 and knows the business well. She's very ....

6 She's good at understanding complicated problems. She's very

....

7 She's a team player. She likes working with her ....

8 She works well in difficult situations. She .... well with stress.

5 **Write a short advert for your own job or a job you'd like to do.**

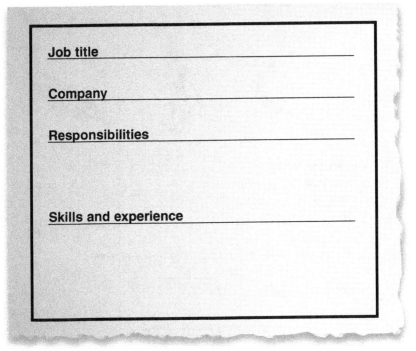

Job title

Company

Responsibilities

Skills and experience

6 **Fill in the gaps.**

| stand   enjoy   fun   go   hopeless   interested |

1 I _enjoy_ playing basketball.

2 I can't .... jogging.

3 I'm .... at horse riding.

4 I'd love to have a .... at elephant polo.

5 I'm not .... in hiking.

6 I think fishing is great ....

9

7 **Complete the puzzle.**

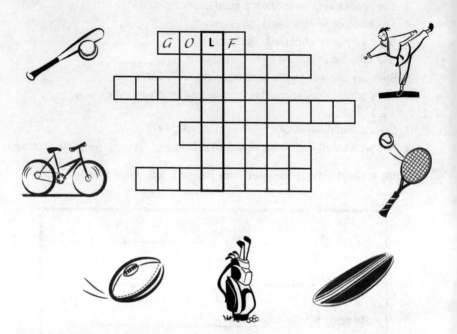

8 **Correct the mistakes.**

1 How goes the work?
   How's the work going?

2 We have problems with the budget on this project.

3 We run two weeks behind schedule at the moment.

4 He enjoys to watch boxing.

5 She's very good in making presentations.

6 Engineers need being analytical.

3 | Choices

1 Make six sentences. Use phrases from each box.

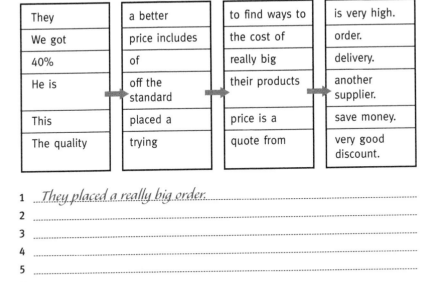

They	a better	to find ways to	is very high.
We got	price includes	the cost of	order.
40%	of	really big	delivery.
He is	off the standard	their products	another supplier.
This	placed a	price is a	save money.
The quality	trying	quote from	very good discount.

1 *They placed a really big order.*

2

3

4

5

6

2 You started a new job last month. Write an email to a colleague from your old company. Compare your new job with your old one or an imaginary one. Write up to 70 words.

To:
From:
Subject: My new job

Hi ...,
Let me tell you a little bit about my new job. My office here is
much bigger ...

3 **Make sentences. Use *as ... as.***

1 This mobile / expensive / that one.
   This mobile is as expensive as that one.

2 The film / not / interesting / the book.
   _____

3 The winter in Alaska / cold / in Siberia.
   _____

4 Some journeys by train / quick / by plane.
   _____

5 The increase in sales / not / big / we wanted.
   _____

6 Our profits this year / not / high / last year.
   _____

4 **Make sentences. Use the superlative.**

1 This is one of __*the most advanced*__ machines in the world.
   (+ advanced)

2 Our warehouse has _____ facilities in the city.
   (+ good)

3 This is one of _____ jobs I do. (– interesting)

4 This is _____ office in the building. (+ bad)

5 _____ people work for us. (+ experienced)

6 Our suppliers produce _____ equipment.
   (– expensive)

7 Their company manufactures _____ cars. (+ fast)

5 **Underline the correct words.**

1 The most *possible* / *important* question is money.
2 It's *compulsory* / *essential* to have reliable colleagues.
3 It's *necessary* / *compulsory* for British Airways pilots to wear uniform.
4 Good IT skills are *essential* / *possible* for this job.
5 I don't think it's *important* / *possible* to increase our profits any more.
6 She made a very *necessary* / *difficult* decision.

6 **Match the pairs to make sentences.**

1 What's the best time   a part of the country?
2 What's the weather   b some good hotels?
3 What are the   c like in the summer?
4 Do you need to have   d of year to visit your country?
5 Can you recommend   e rent a car?
6 Is it cheap to   f a car to travel around?
7 Where's the nicest   g best campsites to go to?

7 **Write the words next to each picture. Then find them in the puzzle.**

A	S	M	E	T	S	T	K
E	F	O	R	E	S	T	A
S	A	U	P	E	R	O	M
S	A	N	K	G	O	C	E
H	B	T	H	B	M	E	H
C	E	A	R	O	L	A	J
A	A	I	S	L	A	N	D
S	C	N	W	E	K	I	Y
C	H	E	R	R	E	K	O

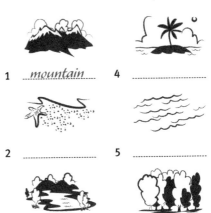

1 _mountain_   4 _____

2 _____   5 _____

3 _____   6 _____

8 **Write a holiday postcard to a friend. Answer these questions: Where are you? When did you arrive? Where are you staying? What is there to see/do? Write up to 70 words.**

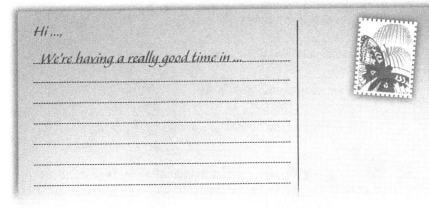

Hi ...,

We're having a really good time in ..._____

_____

_____

_____

_____

_____

9 **Correct the mistakes.**

1 The prices online are cheapest than in this store.
    The prices online are cheaper than in this store.

2 This product is not as good is that one.

    _____

3 I think you have best idea.

    _____

4 That was the most quick journey.

    _____

5 I think the situation is worser now.

    _____

4 | Experience

1 **Fill in the gaps with _be_ in the past simple.**

1 The machine _wasn't_ very safe. It was very dangerous.
2 The sales figures _____ very complicated. They weren't easy to understand.
3 The project _____ a flop. It wasn't successful.
4 The old computers _____ very reliable. They were too slow as well.
5 The bicycle _____ a successful invention. The design wasn't complicated.
6 The running costs _____ very high. The car wasn't very economical.

2 **Rewrite the sentences. Use _too_ or _enough_.**

1 That machine was too complicated. (simple)
  That machine wasn't simple enough.
2 The batteries weren't big enough. (small)
  ----
3 That job was too boring. (interesting)
  ----
4 The old planes weren't safe enough. (dangerous)
  ----
5 The targets were too high. (low)
  ----
6 The report was too difficult to read. (easy)
  ----

3 **You are going to give a short presentation in English about a project you worked on recently. Write notes to help you. Write up to 60 words.**

----

4 **Complete the table.**

Infinitive	Past simple positive	Past simple negative
help	helped	didn't help
	was/were	
		didn't understand
think		
buy		
	made	
		didn't come
	read	
know		
		didn't choose
succeed		
		didn't say

5 **Complete the puzzle. All the words contain the letter 'L'.**

1 It was a very ....*difficult*... job.
2 I couldn't .... the problem.
3 We had lots of .... with the computers.
4 The .... was the low quality.
5 I could see only one .... to the problem.
6 It was .... to open the file.

6 **Find the words. Then match the pairs to make sentences.**

1 minace
2 lame
3 drenagnig
4 daclene
5 cokode
6 poshginp

a I .... a big meal.
b I went ....
c I went to the ...*cinema*... .
d I went out for a ....
e I .... the house.
f I did some ....

15

7 Write an email to a friend saying what you did at the weekend. Write up to 80 words.

To:
From:
Subject: The weekend

Hi ...,
How are things?

8 Correct the mistakes.

1 Yesterday I buyed a new car.
   Yesterday I bought a new car.

2 I speaked to my boss this morning.

3 I weren't able to book a seat.

4 The battery wasn't enough big.

5 He send me an email last week.

6 They wasn't in the office on Friday.

7 The meeting room was to small.

5 | Arrangements

1 **Make five sentences. Use phrases from each circle.**

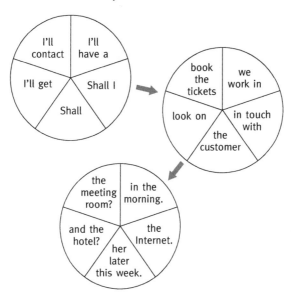

1 *I'll contact the customer in the morning.*
2
3
4
5

2 **You had a meeting with an English colleague. In the meeting you offered to do five things. Write a message confirming what you'll do. Write up to 90 words.**

Dear ...,

3 **Complete the puzzle.**

		1 C	H	E	C	K	
2	K						
3	F						
		4 T					
5	C						
6	B						
7	I						

1 Can you ...*check*... all the details?
2 Could you let me _____ the result?
3 Please _____ attached the document you requested.
4 I'll get in _____ with them.
5 Shall I give you a _____ this afternoon?
6 I'll get _____ to you as soon as possible.
7 Shall I look _____ the flights?

4 **Put the words in order. Make sentences.**

1 find / please / the / the / of / attached / minutes / meeting / team .
..*Please find attached the minutes of the team meeting.*..

2 confirm / I / details / your / the / of / reservation / hotel .
----

3 I'll / discussed, / week / complete / next / as / the / design .
----

4 attach / our / conversation, / list / I / price / the / following / new .
----

5 forward / sales / I / meeting / at / you / to / again / the / look / conference .
----

6 don't / please / to / customer / contact / hesitate / services .
----

5 **Correct the mistakes.**

1 I'll get in touch with her?
..*Shall I get in touch with her? / I'll get in touch with her.*..

2 I have a word with him.
----

3 According to the timetable, the flight is leaving at 10.
----

4 He stays in Paris at the moment.
----

5 As discussed, I'm arrive on Sunday.
----

6 The sales conference happens in Las Vegas this year.
----

6 **Fill in the gaps in the conversations at the tourist information office.**

| information   leaflets   maps   souvenirs   gift   museum   guided |

1

A Morning.

B Good morning.

A Do you have any ...*information*.... about the town?
Any street _____ ? Any _____ ?

B Sure. Here you are.

A Thank you.

2

A Excuse me. Is there a shop near here where they sell _____ ?

B Yes, there are lots of _____ shops in the old town.

A OK, thanks very much.

3

A Is the _____ open today?

B Yes. It's Wednesday today, so it opens at two. There's a
_____ tour then.

7 **You spoke to a colleague on the phone about your visit next week. Now write an email to confirm the arrangements (date, time of meeting, travel and hotel details). Write up to 70 words.**

To:
From:
Subject: Next week's visit

Dear ...,

_____
_____
_____
_____
_____
_____
_____
_____

6 | Objectives

1 **Make five sentences. Use phrases from each box.**

If our forecast	opinion, the	product will probably be	in the long term.
If your idea	it'll definitely	will work	good profit.
I think	is accurate,	be a	very popular.
Perhaps	the idea	the project will	flop.
In my	works, we'll	make a	be a big success.

1 *If our forecast is accurate, the project will be a big success.*

2 ....

3 ....

4 ....

5 ....

2 **Sense or nonsense? Change the nonsense sentences so that they make sense. (Sometimes there is more than one way to do this.)**

		S	N
1	He'll probably finish tomorrow. It's a long-term project.	☐	☑
2	I'll definitely get the job. I did badly in the interview.	☐	☐
3	In the short term, over the next ten years, we'll get the results we need.	☐	☐
4	If we travel the day before, we'll certainly be on time for the meeting.	☐	☐
5	This company's unlikely to win the contract because its prices are high.	☐	☐
6	I think we'll change supplier because he's lowering his prices.	☐	☐

1 *He'll probably finish tomorrow. It's a short-term project. /*
   He probably won't finish tomorrow. It's a long-term project.

....

....

....

....

....

....

3 **Write the first part of the sentences in the continuous form of the verb. Then match the pairs.**

1 We / plan / invest / in new
   We're planning to invest in new

2 He / hope / win
   ----

3 She / aim / improve / her
   ----

4 We / hope / get / good results
   ----

5 They / go / open
   ----

a 50 new stores.

b in the next quarter.

c technology.

d sales by 20%.

e this contract.

4 **Complete the puzzle.**

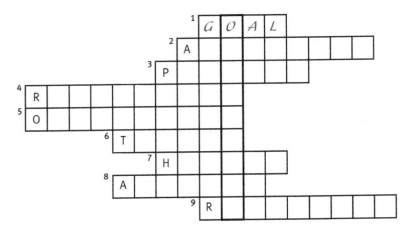

1 Our ..*goal*.. is to increase profits.
2 He wants to be a company director. He's very _____ .
3 I'm meeting the _____ manager on Friday to discuss progress.
4 I don't think the price is too high. In fact, it's very _____ .
5 The company forecasts a 50% increase in sales. I think this is
   _____ .
6 I didn't meet my sales _____ last week.
7 I'm _____ to meet all my targets, but I don't think I'll do it.
8 He doesn't have enough good staff to help him _____ his objectives.
9 His plans aren't _____ . They won't work in practice.

21

5 Write notes to help you give a short presentation on your company's (or an imaginary company's) aims and objectives for the next three months. Talk about costs, sales, staff and new equipment. Write up to 70 words.

We have some very ambitious targets for the next three months ...

----

6 Put the conversation at a travel agency in order. Write 1–11 in the boxes.

☐ When would you like to travel?

☐ Any time in the next two weeks. Are there any cheap flights?

☐ No problem. Visa, American Express or MasterCard?

☐ 1 Hello. Can I help you?

☐ Yes, please. I'd like to book a flight to Rome.

☐ Yes, about 60%. The return flight is only £72.

☐ Let me check. Yes, we have a few last-minute offers for this weekend.

☐ Is there a big discount?

☐ Can I pay by credit card?

☐ Great! Are there any extra charges?

☐ No, everything's included in the fare.

7 Correct the mistakes.

1 I go to the meeting if it starts at 4 o'clock.
   I'll go to the meeting if it starts at 4 o'clock.

2 I don't think the project be successful.

----

3 It's unlikely that he meets his target this month.

----

4 We aim to improve the technology in the next two years.

----

5 We're planning increase sales in Asia.

----

6 She's hoping to getting a refund.

----

7 Maybe he phones us next week.

----

7 | Success

1 **Make questions with *ever*.**

1 have / job in Rome?

Have you ever had a job in Rome?

2 go / Japan?

3 do / IT course?

4 work for / English company?

5 climb / mountain?

6 give / presentation?

2 **Make six sentences. Use phrases from each box.**

I've already interviewed	finished the	agenda so far.
We've already started	three people	jobs.
I've written	work on	email yet.
She hasn't	schedule with all the	report yet.
I haven't replied	half of the	the installation.
We're on	to his	for the job.

1 *I've already interviewed three people for the job.*

2

3

4

5

6

3 **Complete the puzzle.**

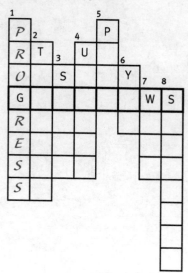

1 We're making good __progress__ with the project.
2 We're having _____ with the installation.
3 It's a very difficult problem to _____ .
4 I gave him an _____ on the situation.
5 Everything is going to _____ .
6 We haven't finished _____ .
7 The work is going _____ .
8 We're two weeks behind _____ .

4 **Find the words and then fill in the gaps.**

ringbo __boring__   sacyr _____   nuf _____
druprsise _____   draces _____
ryzac _____   paphy _____

1 I hate running! It's so __boring__ .
2 He was _____ to drive so fast near a school.
3 Yesterday we went up in a hot air balloon. It was great _____ !
4 I find the idea of parachute jumping very _____ .
5 I was too _____ to swim across the river.
6 I wasn't very _____ when I lost the race.
7 I was _____ at how quickly I learned to sail.

5 **Find verbs in the puzzle to complete the sentences.**

D	I	D	R	K	B	E
R	D	R	I	V	E	N
O	W	E	D	R	E	M
V	A	S	D	O	N	E
E	T	W	E	R	N	K
F	O	U	N	D	F	L
M	A	M	S	W	I	M

1 I've __been__ to Paris many times.
2 I've never _____ a sports car.
3 I've never _____ in the Atlantic.
4 He's _____ the New York marathon.
5 She's _____ across the Alps on a bicycle.
6 They've _____ the best way to keep fit.

6 **Correct the mistakes.**

1 I've just spoke to my boss about my future with the company.
   I've just spoken to my boss about my future with the company.

2 We've be very busy so far this morning.
   ----

3 Have you ever work with him before?
   ----

4 We've yet done everything.
   ----

5 So far I only write the first two pages of the report.
   ----

6 I already repair the machine.
   ----

7 **You are a human resources manager. Write a memo to all staff about the person who has accepted the post of sales manager. Give a few details of his/her education and experience. Write up to 100 words.**

MEMO

To: All staff
Subject: New sales manager
I am pleased to announce that ... _____
_____
_____
_____
_____
_____
_____
_____

8 | Media

1 Write what has happened in the currency markets so far today.

1 £ (+2%) – $ (go up)
The pound has gone up 2% against the dollar.

2 ¥ (–1%) – £ (decrease)

3 € (+1%) – $ (increase)

4 ¥ (–2%) – € (fall)

5 € (+3%) – £ (rise)

6 $ (–4%) – ¥ (go down)

2 Make five sentences. Use phrases from each box.

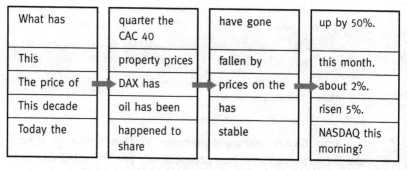

What has	quarter the CAC 40	have gone	up by 50%.
This	property prices	fallen by	this month.
The price of	DAX has	prices on the	about 2%.
This decade	oil has been	has	risen 5%.
Today the	happened to share	stable	NASDAQ this morning?

1 *What has happened to share prices on the NASDAQ this morning?*
2
3
4
5

3 You have to speak briefly in a meeting about the economic situation in your country. Make notes in English to help you give the talk. Talk about currency, property prices, inflation and unemployment. Write up to 60 words.

The economic situation has ...

4 **Complete the puzzle.**

Across ▶

1 The __economic__ situation was very different in the 1950s.
2 Banks _____ money to people.
3 There was a _____ in the property market in 2003.
4 We've borrowed a lot of money, so we now have to pay off the _____ .
5 Sales have started to _____ this quarter.

Down ▼

6 There was a long _____ in America after 1929.
7 You can _____ money from a bank.
8 _____ is high at the moment. A lot of businesses are closing.
9 The interest on our _____ is only 4.6%.
10 The price of oil dropped quickly overnight. There was a _____ .

5 **Put the conversation in the correct order. Number the boxes 1–10.**

- [ ] No, I didn't actually.
- [ ] Well, I wanted to watch my favourite soap and a quiz show.
- [ ] You missed a very interesting programme then. The presenter was brilliant.
- [ ] Yes. It was incredible to hear how he spent a million in four weeks!
- [ ] So you saw the documentary about the Incas?
- [1] Did you watch TV last night?
- [ ] Yes, I watched some really good programmes.
- [ ] Yes, I liked the interview with that American actress.
- [ ] You know I can't stand soap operas. I never watch them. Did you see that late night talk show then?
- [ ] Really? I thought she was boring. For me the best interview was with the quiz show contestant.

6 **Sense or nonsense? Change the nonsense sentences so that they make sense. (Sometimes there is more than one way to do this.)**

	S	N
1 The pound has gone up against the dollar. Yes, the value of the dollar has increased.	[ ]	[✓]
2 House prices are stable. Yes, there's a boom in the property market at the moment.	[ ]	[ ]
3 Have you borrowed a lot of money from the bank? No, I didn't take out any loans.	[ ]	[ ]
4 Are you still working for TMP? Yes. I'm unemployed at the moment.	[ ]	[ ]
5 Did the film have subtitles? Yes, it was dubbed.	[ ]	[ ]
6 Did you see the golf match yesterday? No, I didn't watch the sports channel last night.	[ ]	[ ]

1   The pound has gone down against the dollar. / Yes, the value of the dollar has decreased.

----

1 **Underline the correct answer.**

1 Last week the film *shown* / *is shown* / <u>*was shown*</u> on TV.
2 Recently our products *are advertised* / *were advertised* / *advertised* on the Internet.
3 Our brand *is promoted* / *promoted* / *promotes* on several channels.
4 Product placement *uses* / *is used* / *used* by many companies.
5 Several of our new products *returned* / *were returned* / *are returned*.
6 Most of the parts of this car *is manufactured* / *manufactured* / *are manufactured* in Germany.

2 **Complete the puzzle.**

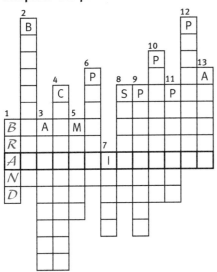

1 We advertise our _brand_ on TV.
2 You can see our adverts on _____ in the street.
3 Is it expensive to _____ in that magazine?
4 Our TV _____ have increased our sales by 30%.
5 We're aiming to improve our _____ share.
6 How do you _____ your brand?
7 Our company has a very good _____ .
8 We _____ a basketball team.
9 I think product _____ is very successful.
10 Our clothes were worn by actors in a TV _____ .
11 Their new sports car was used in a film for a _____ of $10,000.
12 We have a new strategy for the _____ of the brand.
13 _____ is short for advertisement.

3 **Make five sentences. Use phrases from each box.**

He set	a lot of	bankrupt she was	market last year.
After her first	off all of the	money in the stock	our profits.
We tried	hard to cut	workers when the company	left Berghaus Fashions.
We invested	up his business in	costs to increase	unemployed for two years.
They laid	company went	2003 when he	started to lose money.

1 *He set up his business in 2003 when he left Berghaus Fashions.*

2 ....

3 ....

4 ....

5 ....

4 **Sense or nonsense? Change the nonsense sentences so that they make sense. (Sometimes there is more than one way to do this.)**

                                                                        S   N

1 Was your marketing strategy effective?
   Yes, our sales decreased.   ☐   ☑

2 Did your business get better?
   Yes, so we laid off a lot of staff.   ☐   ☐

3 Did you download the details from the company's website?
   Yes, I lost the Internet connection.   ☐   ☐

4 Did you solve your problem?
   No, I found the information on the FAQ page.   ☐   ☐

5 Did you read the online article?
   No, I couldn't because I'm not registered.   ☐   ☐

6 I couldn't log onto the company's web page because I
   forgot my password.   ☐   ☐

1 Yes, our sales increased. / No, our sales decreased.

....

....

....

....

5 Write a short history of your company (or a company you know) for the first page on a company website. Say when it was set up, how it grew and how it developed. Write up to 80 words.

----

6 Put the conversation in the correct order. Number the boxes 1–8.

☐ Did you enter your user name and password correctly?

☐ There must be a problem with the bank's server.

1 What's the matter?

☐ Are you connected?

☐ Yeah, but it's very slow. And yesterday I couldn't log onto my bank account.

☐ Oh ... I'm having problems with the Internet.

☐ Yeah, maybe ... I think I'll give them a call.

☐ Yes, but I got a message that said I wasn't registered.

7 Write the words. Then fill in the gaps.

dragulaly _gradually_   lewl _____   nafilly _____
snedudly _____   snifcangility _____
hrad _____   qulicyk _____

We started to build the business ¹ _gradually_. We didn't want to grow too ² _____ at first. In the early years we worked very ³ _____, but progress was slow. Our best year was in 2003. Sales improved ⁴ _____ and we made huge profits. We continued to do ⁵ _____ until the end of the following year, when demand ⁶ _____ dropped. ⁷ _____, however, the business got better and things are now OK again.

1 **Make six suggestions. Use phrases from each box.**

How could	some new	the name for	new managers?
Why don't we	opening	packaging for	Thailand?
What about	use the plans	stores in	hot countries.
Why not organise	about changing	sent	the Asian market?
Let's design	a training course in	the UK for all	by the Bangkok office?
How	we increase	sales	in Asia?

1 *How could we increase sales in Asia?*

2

3

4

5

6

2 **Fill in the gaps and then put the sentences in order. Number the boxes 1–8.**

☐ If we _____ (can) improve our advertising, we _____ (increase) sales.

☐ If we _____ (double) the number of products we make, we _____ (can) deliver faster.

☐ If we _____ (open) a new production line, we _____ (can) double the number of products we make.

☐ If we _____ (have) more satisfied customers, we _____ (increase) profits.

☐ If we _____ (have) more creative ideas, we _____ (can) improve our advertising.

[1] If we *did* (do) more lateral thinking, we *'d have* (have) more creative ideas.

☐ If we _____ (can) deliver faster, we _____ (have) more satisfied customers.

☐ If we _____ (increase) sales, we _____ (can) open a new production line.

3 Complete the puzzle.

```
                              8
                          1  O  P  T  I  O  N
                          2  W  □  □  □  □  □
                  6
                  C
          3    7
          B  □  □  □  □  I
4
R  □  □  □  □  □  □  □

          5  S  □        □
```

Across ►

1 I think we should choose this __option__ .
2 I'm _____ about Simon, he's working too hard at the moment.
3 What are the _____ of opening a factory in Poland?
4 I wouldn't _____ using that supplier.
5 We have to be _____ before we sign the contract.

Down ▼

6 It's important to _____ all the suggestions.
7 What a very good _____ !
8 That's an interesting _____ . I'll discuss it with my boss.

4 Write the words. Then fill in the gaps.

dragupe __upgrade__   noctecnoni _____   naccle _____
drufen _____   stempelpun _____   laydeed _____

1 Can I __upgrade__ my ticket to business class?
2 The flight was _____ because of technical problems.
3 I'm sorry, I have to _____ the booking.
4 You can have a _____ on first class tickets.
5 I missed my _____ by four minutes.
6 You pay a _____ for meals on some flights.

5 You are on a business trip. You're going to be late for a meeting with a customer because of transport problems. Write a text message explaining what's happened. Say what you're going to do and when you expect to arrive. Write up to 50 words.

I'M GOING TO BE LATE FOR OUR MEETING.

OPTIONS   SELECT   BACK

6 **Correct the mistakes.**

1 If we left now, we can make our connection.

   If we left now, we could make our connection.

2 LH pilots should wear a uniform. It's compulsory.

   ---

3 People who work on building sites shouldn't wear protective clothing.

   ---

4 This is a good product. You shouldn't buy it.

   ---

5 You don't have to speak like that to your boss. Be more polite.

   ---

6 We can improve the design if we had more time.

   ---

11 | Transport

1 Make four sentences. Use phrases from each box.

The best	the building,	a bus here, it'll take	under the river.
If you	leads into	a tunnel, which goes	you to the airport.
To get out of	get on	you have to go	through that exit.
This road	way to get into	the town centre is	to take a taxi.

1   *The best way to get into the town centre is to take a taxi.*

2   ....

3   ....

4   ....

2 Match the pairs to make sentences.

1 Our office is on the top floor. The main reception ————————

2 Can you help me lift up

3 We skied down

4 Go along

5 This high-speed train flies above

6 You need to get off

7 The tourist bus goes around

a the tracks.

b is ten floors below.

c my suitcase, please?

d the mountain together.

e the city.

f the corridor until you get to the lift.

g the train at the next stop.

3 Write the words and then match the opposites.

dewi *wide*   vayhe ....   wol ....

vaboe ....   glith ....   lobew ....

ghih ....   hitck ....   rowran *narrow*

niht ....

wide	narrow

4 **Label the drawings with the words in the box.**

| length   thickness   height   width |

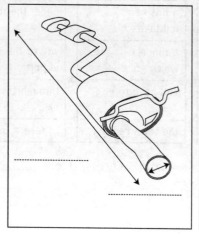 

----

5 **Complete the puzzle.**

1 You must wear _protective_ clothing in the lab.

2 Danger of falling objects! You must wear a _____ _____ at all times.

3 You must wear _____ protection when the aircraft engines are running.

4 Follow the health and safety rules to avoid _____ .

5 There are high levels of dust in the air, so you must wear a _____ .

6 There is a list of health and safety _____ in all areas of the plant.

7 You should wear protective shoes or _____ .

8 High _____ clothes are essential on the tarmac.

9 Use protective _____ when picking up materials.

10 We should all work together to _____ accidents.

6 **Put the conversation in order. Number the boxes 1–12.**

☐ So you had TV in your room?

☐ Great. Have you ever been on a cruise?

☐ Yes, satellite TV. You had to buy a card to watch it. That was the only extra charge. Everything else was free.

☐ No, never.

☐ So you spent a lot of time on deck?

☐ Yes, it was nearly 40 metres long. I couldn't believe it!

☐ It was our first time as well, but the ship was fantastic.

☐ Yes, but there was also a health and fitness club with a sauna.

☐ What did you do in the evenings?

☐ Was there a swimming pool?

☐ *1* How was the holiday then?

☐ Well, after dinner, we usually went to the cabaret bar. The shows were always good. Sometimes we just stayed in the cabin and watched TV.

7 **Write a postcard to a friend. Tell him/her a little bit about the fantastic time you are having on a Caribbean cruise. Write up to 90 words.**

Dear ...,
I'm having a fantastic time here on
my Caribbean cruise!

8 **Fill in the gaps with *must* or *mustn't*.**

1 You __*must*__ have a visa to go to Russia.

2 You _____ carry sharp objects onto a plane.

3 You _____ drink and drive.

4 You _____ be over 17 to take a driving test in the UK.

5 You _____ cross the road when the lights are red.

6 You _____ be a good communicator to make effective presentations.

1 Complete the puzzle.

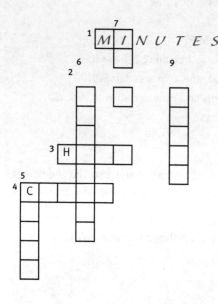

Across ►

1 Have you got a copy of the _minutes_ from the last meeting?

2 Does everybody have an _____?

3 We didn't _____ a meeting to discuss the report.

4 Our new boss likes to _____ all the progress meetings.

Down ▼

5 Details of the meeting were _____ last week.

6 I'd like to send my _____ as I can't make the meeting tomorrow.

7 What's the first _____ on the agenda?

8 Would somebody _____ the minutes, please?

9 Did you _____ the last meeting? I can't remember.

2 Correct the mistakes.

1 I'll phone you until I get to the airport.
   I'll phone you when I get to the airport.

2 We'll ring the office when we'll arrive at the hotel.
   _____

3 I'll phone you as fast as I can.
   _____

4 I won't start the meeting before you'll get here.
   _____

5 She said she be very busy today.
   _____

6 He told me he have a copy of the minutes.
   _____

3 **Make six sentences. Use phrases from each box.**

She promised	keen to be	interviews as he	knows one of the candidates.
They've agreed to	increase	to speak	until Monday.
I've	part in the job	to start the project	new project team.
She said	she was happy	the report two weeks	about health and safety.
I'm very	decided not	part of the	by 20%.
He's reluctant to take	to finish	the budget	ahead of schedule.

1 *She promised to finish the report two weeks ahead of schedule.*
2 ....
3 ....
4 ....
5 ....
6 ....

4 **Write an email to a colleague about a discussion you recently had with a customer. Write about what was discussed and what you both agreed to do. Write up to 100 words.**

> ◻◻◻
>
> **To:**
> **From:**
> **Subject:** Customer meeting
>
> ....
> ....
> ....
> ....
> ....
> ....
> ....
> ....
> ....
> ....

5   **Put the conversations in the correct order. Number the boxes 1–7 and 1–8.**

At reception

☐ Thanks.

☐ No, people are still having coffee in the cafeteria.

☐ Hello, Mr Briggs. Have you come for the strategy meeting?

☐ Yes. I'm sorry I'm late. Has the meeting started?

1̲ Hello, my name's Phil Briggs.

☐ If you'd like to have a seat, I'll ring for someone to get you.

☐ Ah, good.

Before the meeting

☐ Yes, thank you.

☐ Coffee would be great.

☐ Not bad. All the trains were on time today.

☐ No problem, there's a drinks machine just outside in the corridor.

☐ And how was the journey?

1̲ Shall I take your coat?

☐ Great. Thanks.

☐ Really, that makes a change. Can I get you anything to drink?

6   **Choose the best replies.**

1 Hi
   a Hello.   **b** Hi.   **c** Good morning.

2 How are you?
   a Yes, and how are you?   **b** Bad.   **c** Very well, thanks.

3 Sorry I'm late.
   a So am I.   **b** That's OK.   **c** Are you often late?

4 After you.
   a No, ladies before gentlemen.   **b** Thank you.   **c** Yes, please.

5 Would you like a seat?
   a Why?   **b** Yes, please.   **c** Probably.

6 Do you mind if we have a break now?
   a No, not at all.   **b** Yes, I do mind.   **c** Yes.

7 Shall I take your coat?
   a Very good idea!   **b** Yes, thank you.   **c** Where to?

8 Can I get you anything to drink?
   a To drink or not to drink? That is the question.
   b Why?   **c** No, I'm fine thanks.

Transcripts

Unit 1

▶▶ 1 Make sentences.
Listen to the example.

I'm in charge of
customer service
I'm in charge of customer service.

the sales department
I'm in charge of the sales department.

the marketing team
I'm in charge of the marketing team.

I deal with
production problems
I deal with production problems.

financial problems
I deal with financial problems.

difficult customers
I deal with difficult customers.

▶▶ 2 Make negative sentences.
Listen to the example.

I'm an assistant.
I'm not an assistant.

He's in charge of marketing.
He isn't in charge of marketing.

We're responsible for exports.
We aren't responsible for exports.

They're in the meeting room.
They aren't in the meeting room.

They work together.
They don't work together.

She has problems at work.
She doesn't have problems at work.

▶▶ 3 Ask questions.
Listen to the example.

in the office
he	*Is he in the office?*
she	*Is she in the office?*
they	*Are they in the office?*

Where
your offices	*Where are your offices?*
the car park	*Where's the car park?*
the toilets	*Where are the toilets?*

When
the fair start	*When does the fair start?*
the show end	*When does the show end?*
you finish work	*When do you finish work?*

What
you do	*What do you do?*
they make	*What do they make?*
your company manufacture	

What does your company manufacture?

▶▶ 4 Listen to the conversation.

A Good evening.

B *Hello. I have a reservation. The name's Rogers. A table for one.*

A Yes, OK. If you'd like to come this way, please.

B *Thanks.*

A Are you ready to order now?

B *Yes, to start, the tomato soup, please.*

A And what would you like for the main course?

B *For the main course, lamb with peas and carrots, please.*

Listen again and reply for you.

Unit 2

▶▶| 1 Make sentences.
Use the present continuous.
Listen to the example.

work in the office at the moment

I   *I'm working in the office at the moment.*

he   *He's working in the office at the moment.*

she *She's working in the office at the moment.*

we   *We're working in the office at the moment.*

they *They're working in the office at the moment.*

▶▶| 2 Make questions.
Use the present continuous.
Listen to the example.

at the moment
what you work on
What are you working on at the moment?
what she do
What's she doing at the moment?
where they work
Where are they working at the moment?

▶▶| 3 Make questions.
Use the present continuous.
Listen to the example.

work at home
she   *Is she working at home?*
manage the project
you   *Are you managing the project?*
organise the conference
he   *Is he organising the conference?*
write the report
she   *Is she writing the report?*

▶▶| 4 Make sentences.
Listen to the example.

good at
solve problems
he's *He's good at solving problems.*

sell software
they're *They're good at selling software.*
make decisions
I'm   *I'm good at making decisions.*

not very good at
make presentations
I'm   *I'm not very good at making presentations.*
work on big projects
she's *She's not very good at working on big projects.*
sell computers
we're *We're not very good at selling computers.*

like
work in the design team
I   *I like working in the design team.*
interview people
they *They like interviewing people.*
manage people
she *She likes managing people.*

Unit 3

**▶▶ 1 Make comparatives.
Listen to the example.**

cheap	*cheaper*	big	*bigger*
good	*better*	easy	*easier*
small	*smaller*		
bad	*worse*		

**▶▶ 2 Make positive and negative comparatives.
Listen to the example.**

difficult
more difficult   *less difficult*
expensive
more expensive   *less expensive*
popular
more popular   *less popular*
economical
more economical   *less economical*

**▶▶ 3 Make sentences.
Listen to the example.**

planes   fast   trains
Planes are faster than trains.

bikes   slow   cars
Bikes are slower than cars.

PCs   cheap   laptops
PCs are cheaper than laptops.

emails   good   faxes
Emails are better than faxes.

**▶▶ 4 Make positive superlatives.
Listen to the example.**

This is
good office   *This is the best office.*
new member of the team
This is the newest member of the team.
small office   *This is the smallest office.*
unusual design
This is the most unusual design.

▶▶ 5 Listen to a conversation about tourism.

A So, where are you from?

B *I'm from Finland.*

A Oh, what are the best places to visit in your country?

B *I think some of the best parts of the country are in the east. There are lots of lakes and forests there. It's also very beautiful in the north.*

A What are the best towns to visit?

B *Obviously Helsinki. That's the capital. It has lots of museums and beautiful buildings.*

A What's the best time of year to visit?

B *I think the best time is December or January. Everywhere looks beautiful in the snow.*

A And what's the weather like?

B *It's quite hot in the summer and very cold in the winter.*

Listen again and reply about your country.

Unit 4

▶▶ 1 Make sentences. Use the past simple. Listen to the example.

successful   I
I was successful.
popular   it
It was popular.
late   they
They were late.
high   sales
Sales were high.

have a problem   I
I had a problem.
find a solution   we
We found a solution.
go to America   the team
The team went to America.
make a film   they
They made a film.
cost 20 million dollars   the film
The film cost 20 million dollars.
take 12 months   the project
The project took 12 months.

▶▶ 2 Make negative sentences. Use the past simple. Listen to the example.

product   not successful
The product wasn't successful.
car   not economical
The car wasn't economical.
running costs   not high
The running costs weren't high.

▶▶ 3 Make sentences. Listen to the example.

too
the product   expensive
The product was too expensive.
the demand   small
The demand was too small.
the desk   big
The desk was too big.

enough
the vehicle   safe
The vehicle wasn't safe enough.
the design   simple
The design wasn't simple enough.
the market   big
The market wasn't big enough.

▶▶ 4 Make negative sentences. Listen to the example.

We had problems.
We didn't have problems.
The work took a long time.
The work didn't take a long time.
He solved the problem.
He didn't solve the problem.
They finished in December.
They didn't finish in December.

▶▶ 5 Listen to the phone conversation.

A   Hi, how are you today?
B   *Fine, thanks.*
A   Did you have a good weekend?
B   *Yeah, it was good, thanks.*
A   What was the weather like?
B   *It was great. It was nice and warm.*
A   So what did you do on Saturday?
B   *I went shopping in the morning and in the evening I had some friends round and cooked a meal.*
A   And what about Sunday?
B   *I had a lie in and then I cleaned the house.*

Listen again and reply for you.

Unit 5

**▶▶ 1 Offer to do things.
Listen to the example.**

I'll

check on the Internet
I'll check on the Internet.

give them a call   *I'll give them a call.*

look into flights   *I'll look into flights.*

book the hotel   *I'll book the hotel.*

Shall I

phone back at four o'clock
Shall I phone back at four o'clock?

contact the London office
Shall I contact the London office?

send her an email
Shall I send her an email?

Shall we

catch the same train
Shall we catch the same train?

call them tomorrow
Shall we call them tomorrow?

reserve a table for tonight
Shall we reserve a table for tonight?

**▶▶ 2 Make sentences.
Listen to the example.**

at eleven

flight   arrive
The flight arrives at eleven.

conference begin
The conference begins at eleven.

talk   end
The talk ends at eleven.

train   leave   *The train leaves at eleven.*

shop   open   *The shop opens at eleven.*

film   start   *The film starts at eleven.*

**▶▶ 3 Make sentences about
future arrangements. Listen to the
example.**

next month

I   fly to Madrid
I'm flying to Madrid next month.

I   go to the conference
I'm going to the conference next month.

I   visit a customer in Paris
I'm visiting a customer in Paris next month.

I   give a presentation
I'm giving a presentation next month.

**▶▶ 4 Listen to the conversation
in a tourist information office.**

A   Good morning. Can I help you?

B   *Yes, please. Do you have a list of hotels?*

A   Yes, we've got a leaflet with details
of hotels and restaurants.

B   *Great! Do you also have any free
information about the town?*

A   Yes, we have a street map and
a leaflet.

B   *OK, thanks. Is there a shop near here
where they sell souvenirs?*

A   Yes, there are lots of gift shops near
the station.

B   *OK, thanks very much. Oh, just one
more thing. Is the museum open
today?*

A   Yes, it's open every day from 11 am
to 5 pm.

B   *Thank you very much.*

**Listen again and ask for the same
information.**

Unit 6

**▶▶ 1 Make sentences.
Listen to the example.**

I think it'll be

a success	*I think it'll be a success.*
popular	*I think it'll be popular.*
a flop	*I think it'll be a flop.*
difficult	*I think it'll be difficult.*

**▶▶ 2 Make sentences.
Listen to the example.**

They're planning to
use new technology
They're planning to use new technology.
build a spaceship
They're planning to build a spaceship.
develop the technology
They're planning to develop the technology.

We're aiming to
finish the project this year
We're aiming to finish the project this year.
install the equipment this week
We're aiming to install the equipment this week.

They're hoping to
make a big profit
They're hoping to make a big profit.
cut costs
They're hoping to cut costs.

**▶▶ 3 Make sentences.
Listen to the example.**

If the cost is low
there'll be a big demand
If the cost is low, there'll be a big demand.
lots of people will buy tickets
If the cost is low, lots of people will buy tickets.
there'll be lots of space tourists
If the cost is low, there'll be lots of space tourists.

If the product's too expensive
people won't be happy
If the product's too expensive, people won't be happy.
people won't buy it
If the product's too expensive, people won't buy it.

▶▶ 4 Listen to the conversation at a travel agency.

A Good morning. Can I help you?
B *Yes, please. I'd like to book a flight to Madrid.*
A When would you like to travel?
B *Sometime next month.*
A I'll just check to see if there are any cheap flights.
B *Great.*
A Yes, we have a last-minute offer for next weekend. Are you interested?
B *Yes. Is there a big discount?*
A Yes. The return flight is only £80. That's 50% off the normal price.
B *Fine. Are there any extra charges?*
A No, everything's included in the fare.
B *Can I pay by credit card?*
A No problem.

Listen again and play the part of the customer.

Unit 7

▶▶ 1 Make sentences about specific events in the past. Listen to the example.

I joined the company

in 2005
I joined the company in 2005.

last year
I joined the company last year.

a year ago
I joined the company a year ago.

They left the company

in 2004
They left the company in 2004.

last year
They left the company last year.

four years ago
They left the company four years ago.

▶▶ 2 Make sentences about general experiences in the past. Listen to the example.

I've worked

for several companies
I've worked for several companies.

in France and Italy
I've worked in France and Italy.

in the car industry
I've worked in the car industry.

He's worked

in several project teams
He's worked in several project teams.

with lots of difficult people
He's worked with lots of difficult people.

for BP and Shell
He's worked for BP and Shell.

▶▶ 3 Make questions with *ever*. Listen to the example.

Have you ever

work abroad
Have you ever worked abroad?

use this software
Have you ever used this software?

live in another country
Have you ever lived in another country?

go to Tokyo
Have you ever been to Tokyo?

▶▶ 4 Make negative sentences. Listen to the example.

I've worked abroad.
I haven't worked abroad.

I've used PowerPoint before.
I haven't used PowerPoint before.

He's used this software before.
He hasn't used this software before.

We've been here before.
We haven't been here before.

▶▶ 5 Make sentences in the present perfect. Listen to the example.

I've already

send her the report
I've already sent her the report.

start work on the new project
I've already started work on the new project.

solve the problem
I've already solved the problem.

so far

read half of the report
I've read half of the report so far.

interview two people
I've interviewed two people so far.

visit three of the new customers
I've visited three of the new customers so far.

Unit 8

**▶▶| 1 Make sentences.
Listen to the example.**

share prices have risen

today	*Share prices have risen today.*
this week	*Share prices have risen this week.*
this quarter	*Share prices have risen this quarter.*

the index has fallen

this quarter	*The index has fallen this quarter.*
this year	*The index has fallen this year.*
this week	*The index has fallen this week.*

**▶▶| 2 Say the opposite.
Listen to the example.**

Lots of investors bought shares.
sold   *Lots of investors sold shares.*
The euro increased.
decreased   *The euro decreased.*
The pound went down.
went up   *The pound went up.*
The dollar rose against the euro.
fell   *The dollar fell against the euro.*
The Dow Jones fell 5%.
rose   *The Dow Jones rose 5%.*

**▶▶| 3 Make sentences.
Listen to the example.**

very high at the moment
unemployment
Unemployment's very high at the moment.
inflation
Inflation's very high at the moment.
the stock market
The stock market's very high at the moment.

very low at the moment
interest rates
Interest rates are very low at the moment.
prices
Prices are very low at the moment.
shares
Shares are very low at the moment.

**▶▶| 4 Listen to the interview
about television.**

A How often do you watch TV?
B *I watch TV every night.*
A Did you watch TV last night?
B *Yes, I watched TV for two hours.*
A Which channels do you watch most often?
B *I usually watch Channel 1.*
A Do you watch TV programmes in English?
B *Yes, I often watch programmes in English.*
A What TV programmes do you like most?
B *I like quiz shows and the news.*
A Do you like watching films with subtitles?
B *No, I prefer it when they're dubbed.*
A Have you got satellite or cable TV?
B *Yes, I've got satellite TV.*

Listen again and reply for you.

Unit 9

▶▶| 1 Make sentences in the passive. Listen to the example.

used

Product placement   by many companies
Product placement is used by many companies.
Advertising   to promote the brand
Advertising is used to promote the brand.

seen

TV commercials   by millions of viewers
TV commercials are seen by millions of viewers.
Our logo   on billboards in every
                  town
Our logo is seen on billboards in every town.

sold

Our products   online
Our products are sold online.
This watch   for $5,000
This watch is sold for $5,000.

▶▶| 2 Make sentences with adverbs. Listen to the example.

carefully

He planned the strategy
He planned the strategy carefully.
She looked at the figures
She looked at the figures carefully.
They thought about the problem
They thought about the problem carefully.

gradually

They increased sales
They increased sales gradually.
They laid off staff
They laid off staff gradually.
Their profits decreased
Their profits decreased gradually.

▶▶| 3 Listen to the interview about the Internet.

A How often do you use the Internet?
B *I use the Internet every day.*
A What do you use the Internet for?
B *I use it for sending emails.*
A What do you like about the Internet?
B *I like the fact that you can find information easily.*
A What is the biggest problem for you with the Internet?
B *The biggest problem for me is viruses.*
A Are you happy paying for things with your credit card online?
B *I'm happy if I know the site well.*
A Do you ever get software from the Internet?
B *No, but I download music.*

Listen again and reply for you.

Unit 10

▶▶ 1 Make sentences. Listen to the example.

How could we

improve the design
How could we improve the design?

increase profits
How could we increase profits?

improve our advertising
How could we improve our advertising?

What about

changing the colour
What about changing the colour?

putting more CDs in a pack
What about putting more CDs in a pack?

using a new name
What about using a new name?

▶▶ 2 Make sentences. Listen to the example.

I think we should

develop this idea
I think we should develop this idea.

make a decision
I think we should make a decision.

suggest something else
I think we should suggest something else.

We have to

make a decision today
We have to make a decision today.

finish the job on Friday
We have to finish the job on Friday.

find someone for the job
We have to find someone for the job.

We don't have to

sign the contract now
We don't have to sign the contract now.

have a meeting this week
We don't have to have a meeting this week.

employ new staff
We don't have to employ new staff.

▶▶ 3 Listen to a conversation at the station.

A Good morning. Can I help you?

B *Hello. Yes. I've just missed my connection to Manchester.*

A OK, what train were you booked on?

B *The eleven thirty.*

A Can I have a look at your ticket, please? I just want to check that it's valid for the next train.

B *Yes, here you are. When is the next train?*

A At one o'clock ... OK, your ticket's fine. No problem, but obviously you haven't got a seat reservation and the train's very busy.

B *Can I make a reservation now?*

A Yes, that's no problem.

Listen again and play the part of the passenger.

Unit 11

▶▶| 1 Make sentences. Listen to the example.

How wide

the piece of steel
How wide is the piece of steel?
the desk   *How wide is the desk?*
the room   *How wide is the room?*

How thick

the piece of wood
How thick is the piece of wood?
the piece of metal
How thick is the piece of metal?
the piece of plastic
How thick is the piece of plastic?

How heavy

the parcel   *How heavy is the parcel?*
the machine   *How heavy is the machine?*
the laptop   *How heavy is the laptop?*

▶▶| 2 Make sentences. Listen to the example.

You must wear

ear protection
You must wear ear protection.
a mask
You must wear a mask.
high visibility clothing
You must wear high visibility clothing.
protective boots
You must wear protective boots.

You mustn't

smoke in the toilets
You mustn't smoke in the toilets.
run in the corridors
You mustn't run in the corridors.
work without a hard hat
You mustn't work without a hard hat.
drive without a licence
You mustn't drive without a licence.

▶▶| 3 Listen to the conversation at the reception on a cruise ship.

A Hello. How can I help you?

B *Hi. I'd like some information about the evening entertainment.*

A OK, well the show starts at eight thirty. Would you like to book tickets? I think there are still a few left.

B *Yes, please. How much are they?*

A They're free actually. How many would you like?

B *Two, please.*

A Fine. Can I take your room number, please?

B *Yes, it's 201.*

A Thanks. Here you are.

Listen again and play the part of the passenger.

Unit 12

**▶▶ 1 Make sentences.
Listen to the example.**

I'll call you as soon as
I finish the job
I'll call you as soon as I finish the job.
I arrive at the airport
I'll call you as soon as I arrive at the airport.
I get to the station
I'll call you as soon as I get to the station.

I'll phone you before
I make a decision
I'll phone you before I make a decision.
I leave the office
I'll phone you before I leave the office.

I'll ask her when
I see her tomorrow
I'll ask her when I see her tomorrow.
I speak to her on Monday
I'll ask her when I speak to her on Monday.

**▶▶ 2 Make sentences.
Listen to the example.**

They've agreed to
help
They've agreed to help.
sign the contract
They've agreed to sign the contract.
meet us in April
They've agreed to meet us in April.

He's refused to
write that report
He's refused to write that report.
go to the meeting
He's refused to go to the meeting.

She's promised to
write the report
She's promised to write the report.
book the tickets
She's promised to book the tickets.

▶▶ 3 Listen to the conversation at the reception in a company.

A Good morning. Can I help you?
B *Good morning. I've come for a meeting with Mrs Simpson.*
A Can I have your name?
B *My name's Chris Reed from TP Services.*
A She's in a meeting at the moment. Would you like to have a seat?
B *Thanks.*
A Can I get you anything to drink?
B *No, I'm fine, thanks.*
A Shall I take your coat?
B *Thanks.*
A It's quite hot in here. Do you mind if I open this window?
B *No, not at all.*

Listen again and play the part of the visitor.

Answer key

Unit 1

1
1 She's responsible for the marketing department.
2 He manages six technicians.
3 They report to the sales manager.
4 You're in charge of the project.
5 We deal with (the) financial problems.
6 I look after (the) important customers.

2 *Model answer*
Good morning. My name's Brad Sadler. I work for UP Products. I'm a manager. I'm in charge of the sales department and I'm responsible for sales in Europe. I manage ten salespeople and five assistants. I report to the marketing director.

3
1 Where are the factories?
2 They have offices in London and Rome.
3 Our factory isn't near Bristol.
4 Our customers are mainly from Europe.
5 This year there are 300 companies at the trade show.
6 We export our products all over the world.
7 Do you work in London?

4

¹P	R	O	V	I		E			
				²		E	S	I	G	N
³N	E	E	**D**	S					
				⁴		E	L	I	V	E	R
		⁵P	R	O		U	C	E	S

5
1 Our engineers install the equipment and provide a 24-hour service.
2 We supply spare parts to our customers all over the world.
3 We deliver our software products by air.
4 The company exports equipment to its customers in Italy.

6 *Model answer*
Our company manufactures electrical products. We have two factories in Poland and our office is in Warsaw. We export 40% of what we produce and we deliver for free. We have customers all over the world, but our biggest market is the UK.

7

P	A	E	C	O	A	C	C	O	F
S	A	L	A	D	P	A	H	A	O
L	M	E	R	P	P	R	I	P	C
A	K	M	R	O	L	R	C	P	N
E	A	N	O	L	E	B	K	L	P
K	P	O	T	A	T	O	E	A	O
L	E	A	P	M	N	T	N	K	C
A	A	P	L	B	C	H	I	C	K
B	S	I	W	H	B	F	I	S	H

1 potato   2 salad   3 carrot
4 peas   5 lamb   6 apple
7 chicken   8 fish

8
1 book   2 menu   3 main course
4 starter   5 dessert   6 bill

9
1 e   2 h   3 a   4 d   5 g   6 c
7 b   8 f

Unit 2

1
A How's it going? Is the printer working now?

B Yes.

A Good. So, what are you printing at the moment?

B I'm printing a copy of my report.

A OK. Just in time. The man from UPS is waiting in reception.

2
1 Is the engineer repairing the lift?

2 Are the builders working this morning?

3 What are you doing?

4 Are the men from the phone company working today?

5 Is the architect planning the renovation?

6 Are the builders working to schedule?

7 Are you paying a lot for the design changes?

3 *Model answer*

At the moment I'm visiting the London office to check the installation of the new IT network. Good news! They're a day ahead of schedule. This morning the technicians are installing the new software and the engineers are testing the system. The work is going very well.

4
1 communicator   2 creative
3 confident   4 decisions
5 experienced   6 analytical
7 colleagues   8 copes

5 *Model answer*

> **Job title**
> Sales manager
> **Company**
> Santex Chemicals
> **Responsibilities**
> Manage a team of 15 sales staff
> Coordinate sales in Eastern Europe
> Develop contacts with customers in Poland
> **Skills and experience**
> Five years of successful sales experience
> Management experience
> Good team leader
> Excellent IT skills
> Good communication skills in Polish and English (speaking and writing)

6
1 enjoy   2 stand   3 hopeless
4 go   5 interested   6 fun

7

8
1 How's the work going?

2 We're having problems with the budget on this project.

3 We're running two weeks behind schedule at the moment.

4 He enjoys watching boxing.

5 She's very good at making presentations.

6 Engineers need to be analytical.

Unit 3

1
1 They placed a really big order.
2 We got a better quote from another supplier.
3 40% off the standard price is a very good discount.
4 He is trying to find ways to save money.
5 This price includes the cost of delivery.
6 The quality of their products is very high.

2 *Model answer*
Hi ...,
Let me tell you a little bit about my new job. My office here is much bigger and more comfortable than my old one and the view from the window is more interesting – I don't look onto the car park! I only work part-time, so the job is a lot less tiring. My new boss is also much more friendly than Sandra. No surprises there!

3
1 This mobile is as expensive as that one.
2 The film isn't as interesting as the book.
3 The winter in Alaska is as cold as in Siberia.
4 Some journeys by train are as quick as by plane.
5 The increase in sales isn't / wasn't as big as we wanted.
6 Our profits this year aren't as high as last year.

4
1 This is one of the most advanced machines in the world.
2 Our warehouse has the best facilities in the city.
3 This is one of the least interesting jobs I do.
4 This is the worst office in the building.
5 The most experienced people work for us.
6 Our suppliers produce the least expensive equipment.
7 Their company manufactures the fastest cars.

5
1 important   2 essential
3 compulsory   4 essential
5 possible   6 difficult

6
1 d   2 c   3 g   4 f   5 b
6 e   7 a

7

A	S	M	E	T	S	T	K
E	F	O	R	E	S	T	A
S	A	U	P	E	R	O	M
S	A	N	K	G	O	C	E
H	B	T	H	B	M	E	H
C	E	A	R	O	L	A	J
A	A	I	S	L	A	N	D
S	C	N	W	E	K	I	Y
C	H	E	R	R	E	K	O

1 mountain   2 beach   3 lake
4 island   5 ocean   6 forest

8 *Model answer*
Hi ...,
We're having a really good time in Chester. The weather's great – sunny and warm. We arrived late on Friday evening and went straight to the hotel. We're staying in a really nice hotel in the centre of town. Chester is a really beautiful place. There are lots of things to do. It's perfect if you like shopping, of course. But there's also the cathedral and a museum. See you soon.

9
1 The prices online are cheaper than in this store.
2 This product is not as good as that one.
3 I think you have the best idea.
4 That was the quickest journey.
5 I think the situation is worse now.

Unit 4

1
1 wasn't 2 were 3 was
4 weren't 5 was 6 were

2
1 That machine wasn't simple enough.
2 The batteries were too small.
3 That job wasn't interesting enough.
4 The old planes were too dangerous.
5 The targets weren't low enough.
6 The report wasn't easy enough to read.

3 *Model answer*
Last year I worked in a team of four engineers on the installation of a new production line in our factory. We had lots of trouble with the design because there wasn't much space available. It took a long time to solve the problem and as a result the project wasn't completed on schedule.

4

Infinitive	Past simple positive	Past simple negative
help	helped	didn't help
be	was/were	wasn't/weren't
understand	understood	didn't understand
think	thought	didn't think
buy	bought	didn't buy
make	made	didn't make
come	came	didn't come
read	read	didn't read
know	knew	didn't know
choose	chose	didn't choose
succeed	succeeded	didn't succeed
say	said	didn't say

5
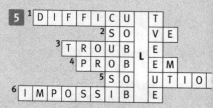

6
1 cinema c 2 meal d
3 gardening f 4 cleaned e
5 cooked a 6 shopping b

7 *Model answer*
Hi ...,
How are things? How was your weekend? We had a really busy time. We went to the cinema on Friday evening and saw that new film with Angelina Roberts and then we went out for a meal. We didn't get home till after 12, so we had a lie in on Saturday. Then we spent the afternoon shopping. In the evening we had some friends round for dinner, so another late night! On Sunday we just relaxed. We did a bit of gardening and then went for a walk.
See you soon,

8
1 Yesterday I bought a new car.
2 I spoke to my boss this morning.
3 I wasn't able to book a seat.
4 The battery wasn't big enough.
5 He sent me an email last week.
6 They weren't in the office on Friday.
7 The meeting room was too small.

Unit 5

1
1 I'll contact the customer in the morning.
2 I'll have a look on the Internet.
3 Shall I book the tickets and the hotel?
4 Shall we work in the meeting room?
5 I'll get in touch with her later this week.

2 *Model answer*

Dear ...,

It was nice to meet you again. I think we had a very useful meeting. I'm writing to confirm what we discussed. I'll book a meeting room at a hotel for the 23rd July and I'll reserve a table for six at a restaurant for lunch. I'll contact some suppliers and ask them to send us their brochures. I'll email the details to everyone as soon as possible and I'll also send you a copy of the latest progress report.

I look forward to seeing you again soon.

Regards,

3

1	C	H	E	C	K
2 K	N	O	W		
3 F	I	N	D		
	4 T	O	U	C	H
5 C	A	L	L		
6 B	A	C	K		
7 I	N	T	O		

4
1 Please find attached the minutes of the team meeting.
2 I confirm the details of your hotel reservation.
3 As discussed, I'll complete the design next week.

4 Following our conversation, I attach the new price list.
5 I look forward to meeting you again at the sales conference.
6 Please don't hesitate to contact customer services.

5
1 Shall I get in touch with her? / I'll get in touch with her.
2 I'll have a word with him. / Shall I have a word with him?
3 According to the timetable, the flight leaves at 10.
4 He's staying in Paris at the moment.
5 As discussed, I'm arriving on Sunday.
6 The sales conference is happening in Las Vegas this year.

6
1 information, maps, leaflets
2 souvenirs, gift
3 museum, guided

7 *Model answer*

Dear ...,

Just a quick note to confirm the arrangements for our next meeting. It's on Tuesday 14th May at 10 am. We're meeting in the Grafton Room at the Bristol Hotel in the centre of Birmingham. The hotel is in New Street, about two minutes' walk from the station. I think the best way to travel is by train.

I attach a map of the town centre for your information.

Regards,

Unit 6

1
1 If our forecast is accurate, the project will be a big success.
2 If your idea works, we'll make a good profit.
3 I think it'll definitely be a flop.

4 Perhaps the idea will work in the long term.

5 In my opinion, the product will probably be very popular.

2 1 N 2 N 3 N 4 S 5 S 6 N

1 He'll probably finish tomorrow. It's a short-term project. / He probably won't finish tomorrow. It's a long-term project.

2 I'll definitely get the job. I did well in the interview. / I definitely won't get the job. I did badly in the interview.

3 In the long term, over the next ten years, we'll get the results we need.

6 I think we'll change supplier because he's increasing / putting up his prices.

3 1 c 2 e 3 d 4 b 5 a

1 We're planning to invest in new technology.

2 He's hoping to win this contract.

3 She's aiming to improve her sales by 20%.

4 We're hoping to get good results in the next quarter.

5 They're going to open 50 new stores.

4

```
1 G O A L
2 A M B I T I O U S
3 P R O J E C T
4 R E A S O N A B L E
5 O P T I M I S T I C
6 T A R G E T
7 H O P I N G
8 A C H I E V E
9 R E A L I S T I C
```

5 *Model answer*

We have some very ambitious targets for the next three months. Our main aim is to increase sales by 15%. We are also aiming to cut

costs by 10%. We are planning to install the new computers and train all our assistants to use the new software by the end of the month. At the moment I see no reason why we won't achieve all our objectives this quarter.

6 1 Hello. Can I help you?

2 Yes, please. I'd like to book a flight to Rome.

3 When would you like to travel?

4 Any time in the next two weeks. Are there any cheap flights?

5 Let me check. Yes, we have a few last-minute offers for this weekend.

6 Is there a big discount?

7 Yes, about 60%. The return flight is only £72.

8 Great! Are there any extra charges?

9 No, everything's included in the fare.

10 Can I pay by credit card?

11 No problem. Visa, American Express or MasterCard?

7 1 I'll go to the meeting if it starts at 4 o'clock.

2 I don't think the project will be successful.

3 It's unlikely that he'll meet his target this month.

4 We're aiming to improve the technology in the next two years.

5 We're planning to increase sales in Asia.

6 She's hoping to get a refund.

7 Maybe he'll phone us next week.

Unit 7

1
1 Have you ever had a job in Rome?
2 Have you ever been to Japan?
3 Have you ever done an IT course?
4 Have you ever worked for an English company?
5 Have you ever climbed a mountain?
6 Have you ever given a presentation?

2
1 I've already interviewed three people for the job.
2 We've already started work on the installation.
3 I've written half of the agenda so far.
4 She hasn't finished the report yet.
5 I haven't replied to his email yet.
6 We're on schedule with all the jobs.

3

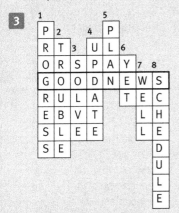

4
1 boring　2 crazy　3 fun　4 scary
5 scared　6 happy　7 surprised

5

D	I	D	R	K	B	E
R	O	R	I	V	E	N
O	W	E	D	R	E	M

E	T	W	E	R	N	K
F	O	U	N	D	F	L
M	A	M	S	W	I	M

1 been　2 driven　3 swum
4 done　5 ridden　6 found

6
1 I've just spoken to my boss about my future with the company.
2 We've been very busy so far this morning.
3 Have you ever worked with him before?
4 We've already done everything.
5 So far I've only written the first two pages of the report.
6 I've already repaired the machine.

7 *Model answer*
I am pleased to announce that Bill Stoneham has accepted the post of sales manager. Bill will start on 1st September. He has over eight years' sales experience, including four years' experience in management. He has worked in Spain and in France. He studied French and Spanish at Manchester University and graduated in 1992. He did a part-time Masters in Business Management three years later. He joined Parabola in Madrid in 1997 as a trainee sales assistant and was promoted to assistant sales manager four years later. He left Parabola in 2002 and joined Uniset in Toulon as an area sales manager.

Unit 8

1

1 The pound has gone up 2% against the dollar.

2 The yen has decreased 1% against the pound.

3 The euro has increased 1% against the dollar.

4 The yen has fallen 2% against the euro.

5 The euro has risen 3% against the pound.

6 The dollar has gone down 4% against the yen.

2

1 What has happened to share prices on the NASDAQ this morning?

2 This quarter the CAC 40 has risen 5%.

3 The price of oil has been stable this month.

4 This decade property prices have gone up by 50%.

5 Today the DAX has fallen by about 2%.

3 *Model answer*

The economic situation has improved considerably over the past 12 months. The value of the euro has risen against most other currencies.

Property prices have gone up 5%. Mortgage rates are at an all-time low. They have fallen by 4% over the year and are now at 2.5%. Inflation has decreased to 1.5%. Unemployment has fallen to just over 4%.

4

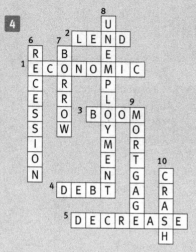

5

1 Did you watch TV last night?

2 Yes, I watched some really good programmes.

3 So you saw the documentary about the Incas?

4 No, I didn't actually.

5 You missed a very interesting programme then. The presenter was brilliant.

6 Well, I wanted to watch my favourite soap and a quiz show.

7 You know I can't stand soap operas. I never watch them. Did you see that late night talk show then?

8 Yes, I liked the interview with that American actress.

9 Really? I thought she was boring. For me the best interview was with the quiz show contestant.

10 Yes. It was incredible to hear how he spent a million in four weeks!

6 1 N 2 N 3 S 4 N 5 N 6 S

1 The pound has gone down against the dollar. / Yes, the value of the dollar has decreased.

2 House prices have risen / gone up.

4 No. I'm unemployed at the moment. / Yes. I'm still working for TMP.

5 No, it was dubbed.

Unit 9

1 1 was shown 2 were advertised
3 is promoted 4 is used
5 were returned
6 are manufactured

2

```
 2                              12
 B                              P
 I                              R
 L                  10          O
 L    4      6      P      13
 B    C      P    8 9 R 11 M  A
 1    O      R      S P O P O  D
 B A A M M   O      P L G A T  V
 R R D M A O 7      O A R Y I  E
 A D V E R T I S E  N C A M O  R
 N S E R K E M O M  A D V E R T I S E M E N T
 D   R C E   A R E  E T
     T I T   G      N T
     I A     E      T
     S L
     E S
```

3
1 He set up his business in 2003 when he left Berghaus Fashions.

2 After her first company went bankrupt she was unemployed for two years.

3 We tried hard to cut costs to increase our profits.

4 We invested a lot of money in the stock market last year.

5 They laid off all of the workers when the company started to lose money.

4 1 N 2 N 3 N 4 N 5 S 6 S

1 Yes, our sales increased. / No, our sales decreased.

2 Yes, so we hired a lot of staff. / No, so we laid off a lot staff.

3 No, I lost the Internet connection.

4 Yes, I found the information on the FAQ page.

5 *Model answer*
Connect 4 was set up in 1993. Over the next two years, the company successfully increased sales of its DIY products and opened two more stores in the Midlands. In 1995 the company expanded rapidly. It developed a website and started online sales with deliveries from its warehouse in Walsall. The online business was a great success and in 2001 warehouses were built in France, Germany and Italy to deal with online orders in Europe.

6
1 What's the matter?

2 Oh ... I'm having problems with the Internet.

3 Are you connected?

4 Yeah, but it's very slow. And yesterday I couldn't log onto my bank account.

5 Did you enter your user name and password correctly?

6 Yes, but I got a message that said I wasn't registered.

7 There must be a problem with the bank's server.

8 Yeah, maybe ... I think I'll give them a call.

7 1 gradually 2 quickly 3 hard
4 significantly 5 well
6 suddenly 7 Finally

Unit 10

1
1 How could we increase sales in Asia?
2 Why don't we use the plans sent by the Bangkok office?
3 What about opening stores in Thailand?
4 Why not organise a training course in the UK for all new managers?
5 Let's design some new packaging for hot countries.
6 How about changing the name for the Asian market?

2
1 If we did more lateral thinking, we'd have more creative ideas.
2 If we had more creative ideas, we could improve our advertising.
3 If we could improve our advertising, we'd increase sales.
4 If we increased sales, we could open a new production line.
5 If we opened a new production line, we could double the number of products we make.
6 If we doubled the number of products we make, we could deliver faster.
7 If we could deliver faster, we'd have more satisfied customers.
8 If we had more satisfied customers, we'd increase profits.

4
1 upgrade   2 delayed   3 cancel
4 refund   5 connection
6 supplement

5   *Model answer*
I'm going to be late for our meeting. Sorry. My train to London was delayed by half an hour. I'm going to get a taxi now, so I hope to be at your office in 15 minutes. Many apologies.

6
1 If we left now, we could make our connection.
2 LH pilots have to wear a uniform. It's compulsory.
3 People who work on building sites should wear protective clothing.
4 This is a good product. You should buy it.
5 You shouldn't speak like that to your boss. Be more polite.
6 We could improve the design if we had more time.

3

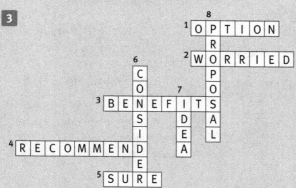

Unit 11

1
1 The best way to get into the town centre is to take a taxi.
2 If you get on a bus here, it'll take you to the airport.
3 To get out of the building, you have to go through that exit.
4 This road leads into a tunnel, which goes under the river.

2
1 b   2 c   3 d   4 f
5 a   6 g   7 e

3
wide – narrow   heavy – light
low – high   above – below
thick – thin

4

5

6
1 How was the holiday then?
2 Great. Have you ever been on a cruise?
3 No, never.
4 It was our first time as well, but the ship was fantastic.
5 Was there a swimming pool?
6 Yes, it was nearly 40 metres long. I couldn't believe it!
7 So you spent a lot of time on deck?
8 Yes, but there was also a health and fitness club with a sauna.
9 What did you do in the evenings?
10 Well, after dinner, we usually went to the cabaret bar. The shows were always good. Sometimes we just stayed in the cabin and watched TV.
11 So you had TV in your room?
12 Yes, satellite TV. You had to buy a card to watch it. That was the only extra charge. Everything else was free.

7 *Model answer*
Dear ...,

I'm having a fantastic time here on my Caribbean cruise! Everything is perfect – the weather, the ship, the food – everything. The facilities on the ship are first class. There's a 50 metre swimming pool on deck, a jogging track and a fitness centre. There's entertainment every evening with shows and cabarets and there are four restaurants with excellent food and service. My cabin is a dream. It even has a jacuzzi and a sauna. I've taken lots of photos, so I can show you everything when I get back.

8
1 must   2 mustn't   3 mustn't
4 must   5 mustn't   6 must

Unit 12

1

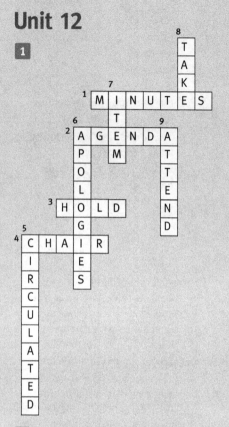

2
1 I'll phone you when I get to the airport.
2 We'll ring the office when we arrive at the hotel.
3 I'll phone you as soon as I can.
4 I won't start the meeting before you get here.
5 She said she was very busy today.
6 He told me he had a copy of the minutes.

3
1 She promised to finish the report two weeks ahead of schedule.
2 They've agreed to increase the budget by 20%.
3 I've decided not to start the project until Monday.

4 She said she was happy to speak about health and safety.
5 I'm very keen to be part of the new project team.
6 He's reluctant to take part in the job interviews as he knows one of the candidates.

4 *Model answer*
Dear ...,
My trip to Liverpool last week went well. I visited the office of DP Systems on Tuesday and met the new head buyer there. She's very interested in developing a new website for her company. She asked lots of questions about prices and schedules. I agreed to send her a detailed specification next week and she said she would email me with some dates when she could come and visit us. She wants to meet the design team to discuss the project in more detail. I'll let you know how things progress.

5 <u>At reception</u>
1 Hello, my name's Phil Briggs.
2 Hello, Mr Briggs. Have you come for the strategy meeting?
3 Yes. I'm sorry I'm late. Has the meeting started?
4 No, people are still having coffee in the cafeteria.
5 Ah, good.
6 If you'd like to have a seat, I'll ring for someone to get you.
7 Thanks.

<u>Before the meeting</u>
1 Shall I take your coat?
2 Yes, thank you.
3 And how was the journey?
4 Not bad. All the trains were on time today.

5 Really, that makes a change.
Can I get you anything to drink?

6 Coffee would be great.

7 No problem, there's a drinks
machine just outside in the
corridor.

8 Great. Thanks.

6 1 b   2 c   3 b   4 b   5 b   6 a
7 b   8 c

Irregular verbs

Infinitive	Past simple	Past participle
be	was/were	been
become	became	become
begin	began	begun
break	broke	broken
bring	brought	brought
build	built	built
buy	bought	bought
catch	caught	caught
choose	chose	chosen
come	came	come
cost	cost	cost
cut	cut	cut
do	did	done
draw	drew	drawn
drink	drank	drunk
drive	drove	driven
eat	ate	eaten
fall	fell	fallen
feel	felt	felt
find	found	found
fly	flew	flown
forget	forgot	forgotten
get	got	got
give	gave	given
go	went	gone
have	had	had
hear	heard /hɜːd/	heard /hɜːd/
keep	kept	kept
know	knew	known
learn	learned/learnt	learned/learnt
leave	left	left
lose	lost	lost
make	made	made
meet	met	met
pay	paid	paid
put	put	put

Irregular verbs

Infinitive	Past simple	Past participle
read	read /red/	read /red/
ring	rang	rung
run	ran	run
say	said	said
see	saw	seen
sell	sold	sold
send	sent	sent
sing	sang	sung
sleep	slept	slept
speak	spoke	spoken
spend	spent	spent
stand	stood	stood
swim	swam	swum
take	took	taken
teach	taught	taught
tell	told	told
think	thought	thought
throw	threw	thrown
understand	understood	understood
wake	woke	woken
wear	wore	worn
win	won	won
write	wrote	written

Acknowledgements

The authors would like to acknowledge above all the significant contribution to the course made by Nathalie and Aimy Ibbotson, and Evgenia Miassoedova. They were a constant source of support and ideas at all stages of the project and displayed remarkable patience!

Thanks also to: Will Capel for believing in the project and for his advice and expertise during the critical early stages of development, Sally Searby for her encouragement and commitment to getting the best out of the course, Clare Abbott for her excellent editorial input – especially in guiding the material through key improvements to the concept and methodology, Elin Jones for her valuable editorial advice, ideas and positive support – much appreciated during the intense phase of writing the first level, and Chris Capper for his helpful input on the early units. A big thanks to our editor Nick Robinson, whose positive energy, ideas and feel for the material have been instrumental in shaping the second level. And a special thanks to our copy editor Fran Banks, for giving *Business Start-up* the benefit of her expertise, eagle eyes and extremely hard work. Additional thanks to Alison Silver for her contribution to Workbook 2.

We would also like to thank the many reviewers who have offered valuable comments on the material at various stages of development, including Alex Case, Helen Forrest, Radoslaw Lewandowski, Rosemary Richey and Robert Szulc.

The publishers would like to thank James Richardson and The Soundhouse Studio for the audio production and Bee2 Ltd for the CD-ROM development.

CD-ROM / Audio CD instructions

Audio CD instructions

Play the CD in a standard CD player. You can also play the CD on your computer:

1 Insert the disc into your CD-ROM drive.
2 The CD-ROM application will open automatically – if you do not want to run the application, close or minimise it.
3 Open your computer's CD player software (for example, Microsoft® Windows Media® Player).

CD-ROM instructions for PC

1 Insert the CD into your CD-ROM drive.
2 The program should start automatically.
3 If, after a few seconds, the program has not started, open 'My Computer', then browse to your CD-ROM drive and double-click on the 'START-UP' icon.

CD-ROM instructions for Mac OSX

1 Insert the CD into your CD-ROM drive.
2 Open the CD-ROM folder and double-click on the 'START-UP' icon.

System requirements

For PC

Recommended: Windows 2000 or XP, 400MHz processor or faster, with 128MB of RAM or more.

For Mac

Essential: Mac OSX, version 10.1 or higher.
Recommended: 400MHz G3 processor or better, with 128MB RAM or more.